winter 2003

winter 2003

TABLE OF CONTENTS

left to right ➡

Introduction

Congratulations on getting your hands on the 4th installment of TOKYOPOP Sneaks!
For those who are new to manga, we bid you welcome! If you are already in the know, welcome back!
This book is a compilation of carefully selected pages that is designed to give you a taste of TOKYOPOP's latest titles. Whether your preference is action or romance, this book is your key to the world of manga. Within these pages you will discover an extraordinary selection of hand-picked titles that will stimulate the senses and capture the imagination. Compared to traditional comic books, TOKYOPOP's manga titles go beyond the ordinary and offer the reader stories with a level of maturity and depth of character that is sure to be appreciated.

TOKYOPOP® Inc. is the leading North American publisher of manga, the fastest growing segment in the publishing industry. With exclusive rights to hundreds of licensed and original book, video and music properties, the company has rapidly become a media convergence leader. TOKYOPOP® has millions of books in print and publishes many hit manga series, including *Love Hina, Chobits, Rave Master, Initial D, GTO, Battle Royale, Cowboy Bebop.* The company created Cine-Manga, releasing titles such as *Finding Nemo, SpongeBob SquarePants, Lizzie McGuire, Spy Kids 2, Kim Possible, Jackie Chan Adventures, TRANSFORMERS Armada,* and *G.I. Joe Spy Troops.* TOKYOPOP® television properties include *Reign: The Conqueror,* and the upcoming *Rave Master,* airing on Cartoon Network in the summer of 2004.

Introduction:

The nexus of L.A. vice and hip-hop life is @Large, an internet gaming cafe with a notorious recording studio upstairs. Everyone comes together in the gaming lounges of @Large—geeks, rappers, techno-ninjas, thugs, wannabees and undercover cops. As one group of kids, known as DNA, attempts to navigate through the trials of adolescence and gain street credibility, they encounter agents of the dark power behind the recording studio. Soon, the DNA crew find themselves fighting for their lives and for the very survival of their community.

Created by: Ahmed Hoke

Ahmed Hoke is a multi-talented illustrator with roots in the L.A. graffiti art scene and a college education in the graphic arts. Ahmed enjoys listening to and producing Hip-Hop music, which has been an inspirational tool for him throughout the years.

Features:

The World's First Hip-Hop Manga!
Street life from a real perspective

Genre
Action/Comedy
SRP: $9.99
Release date: Vol. 1 - 12/09/03

4

I KNOW YOUR NAME, HOMES!
WHAT THE.. POURING 40 OZ ON MY HEAD!
SO NOW YOU'RE MAD.
NAW, I AIN'T MAD!

TO BE CONTINUED...

14

Princess ai

Courtney Love & D.J. Milky
put their spin on celebrity and fantasy.

Manga coming in Summer of 2004

TOKYOPOP®

SHUTTERBOX

Introduction:

When Megan Amano dreams, she travels to a place called Merridiah University, one of the afterlife's premier educational institutes. There she studies as an exchange student, learning the skills necessary to become a living muse. Traditionally, only spirits attend the University, where they are educated before being reborn into the world of the living. However, Megan is still alive. She attends college in Santa Monica, California by day and Merridiah University at night. One day, she finds mysterious pictures from the dream world in her digital camera. They reveal a mystery so deep that Megan is compelled to question her very existence and set forth on a quest to find the answers.

Genre
Romance/Fantasy
SRP: $9.99
Release date:

Created by: Studio Tavicat

Tavisha Wolfgarth-Simons and Rikki Simons met at Disneyland in February of 1990 and were married on October 31, 1994. Both were magically touched by the wonder of Japanese manga at a young age and they have created several American manga-influenced comics such as *Sushi Girl*, and *Reality Check!*

Features:

Appeals to fans of *Under The Glass Moon!*

Studio Tavicat is TOKYOPOP's best-selling U.S.-based manga creator team

Vol. 1 - 10/07/03 Vol. 2 - 01/13/04
Vol. 3 - 05/04/04 Vol. 4 - 09/14/04

As I edged closer...the figure moved on calmly into the darkening pit of the waters.

Why?

When I saw him... if I really saw him... I felt compelled to move closer... mesmerized by his presence.

Yet...I felt I wasn't supposed to be there. The underlying sense was that something here was terribly wrong... a desperation, a silent cry for help.

SHUTTER BOX

TO BE CONTINUED...

26

Introduction:

Han has always had trouble relating to women, but when he plays a new game called World of Hartz he finds himself involved in a totally-immersive gaming experience that turns him into an online hero and an instant hit with all the virtual ladies. Han's growing reputation as the best Hartz player leads to a job offer from the game developer. Once inside, Han finds out that there is a lot more going on than fun, games and chasing girls. A web of power, politics and international conspiracies—plus a game so addictive that it destroys lives—add up to the ultimate challenge for Han as he fights to save his friends and his world.

Created by: Terrence Walker

Terrence Walker started drawing comics in the late 80's for small local newspapers in Arizona. He has become a front-runner in the realm of independent animation. His notoriety throughout the CG community has lead to various discussions with Japanese studios involving anime projects aimed specifically at the Asian market.

Features:

A TOKYOPOP U.S. exclusive manga release!

From the creator of *Anime: Concept to Reality*

A riveting story based on video game culture

Genre
Action/Sci-Fi

SRP: $9.99

Release date: Vol. 1 - 11/04/03

31

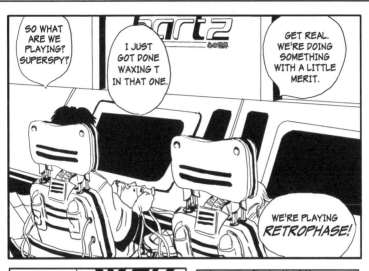

TO BE CONTINUED...

TOKYOPOP® SNEAKS

winter 2003

Cover Art & Graphic Design - Christian Lownds and Chy Lin
Graphic Design - Chy Lin
Project Coordinator - Jason Alnas
Managing Editor - Jill Freshney
Production Coordinator - Antonio DePietro
Production Managers - Jennifer Miller, Mutsumi Miyazaki
Art Director - Matt Alford
Editorial Director - Jeremy Ross
VP of Production - Ron Klamert
President & C.O.O. - John Parker
Publisher & C.E.O. - Stuart Levy

Email: editor@TOKYOPOP.com
Come visit us online at www.TOKYOPOP.com

A **TOKYOPOP** Manga

5900 Wilshire Blvd., Suite 2000, Los Angeles, CA 90036

Baby Birth
© 2001 Sukehiro Tomita and Haruhiko Mikimoto.

Gakuen Tokkei Duklyon
© 2001 by Clamp.

FLCL
© GAINAX, Hajime Ueda.

Forbidden Dance
© 1998 Hinako Ashihara.

Miyuki-chan in Wonderland
©2001 by Clamp.

Planetes
© Makoto Yukimura.

Shirahime-Syo
© 2001 by Clamp.

ShutterBox
© 2003 Rosearik Rikki Simons and Tavisha Wolfgarth-Simons.

World of Hartz
© 2003 by Terrence Walker and TOKYOPOP.

@Large
© 2003 by Laurence Ahmed Hoke and TOKYOPOP.

English text © 2003 by TOKYOPOP.
TOKYOPOP Sneaks is published for promotional use only.

ISBN: 1-59182-408-7

First TOKYOPOP® printing: December 2003

10 9 8 7 6 5 4 3 2 1
Printed in the USA

CREDITS

TOKYOPOP® SNEAKS
winter 2003

TABLE OF CONTENTS

← right to left

Introduction

Congratulations on getting your hands on the 4th
installment of TOKYOPOP Sneaks!
For those who are new to manga, we bid you welcome!
If you are already in the know, welcome back!
This book is a compilation of carefully selected
pages that is designed to give you a taste of
TOKYOPOP's latest titles. Whether your preference is
action or romance, this book is your key to the world
of manga. Within these pages you will discover an
extraordinary selection of hand-picked titles that
will stimulate the senses and capture the imagination. Compared to traditional comic books,
TOKYOPOP's manga titles go beyond the ordinary and
offer the reader stories with a level of maturity and
depth of character that is sure to be appreciated.

TOKYOPOP® Inc. is the leading North American publisher of manga, the fastest growing segment in the
publishing industry. With exclusive rights to hundreds of licensed and original book, video and music
properties, the company has rapidly become a media
convergence leader. TOKYOPOP® has millions of books
in print and publishes many hit manga series,
including *Love Hina, Chobits, Rave Master, Initial
D, GTO, Battle Royale, Cowboy Bebop.* The company
created Cine-Manga, releasing titles such as *Finding
Nemo, SpongeBob SquarePants, Lizzie McGuire, Spy
Kids 2, Kim Possible, Jackie Chan Adventures,
TRANSFORMERS Armada,* and *G.I. Joe Spy Troops.*
TOKYOPOP® television properties include *Reign: The
Conqueror,* and the upcoming *Rave Master,* airing on
Cartoon Network in the summer of 2004.

BABY BIRTH

Introduction:

An ancient seal has been broken, sending a flood of demons into the mortal realm. Hizuru Oborozuki and Takuya Hijou, descendants of the great savior who banished the demons in the past, must fight the evil spirits using their mystical powers. In order to give the world a fighting chance, Takuya uses his music to transform Hizuru into a beautiful warrior. Some things are worth fighting for, but is the Earth one of them? Created with the talents of artist Haruhiko Mikimoto (*Macross*) and writer Sukehiro Tomita.

Created by: Sukehiro Tomita
Haruhiko Mikimoto

Artist Haruhiko Mikimoto is known for his character designs for *Super Dimensional Fortress Macross*, *Aim for the Top* and also producing the hugely popular manga, *Macross 7 Trash*. Writer Sukehiro Tomita is know for his work on the anime of *Beautiful Warrior Sailor Moon*, *Salary Man: Kintaro*, and manga such as *Legend of the Love Angel: Wedding Peach!*

Features:

From the creator of *Robotech*

English adaptation by Jim Krueger, Author of *Earth X*

Release date: Vol. 1 - 09/16/03
Vol. 2 - 11/04/03

Genre
Action/Adventure

SRP: $9.99

T
TEEN
AGE 13+

6

ALL RIGHT! EVERYONE OFF THE RINK!

HIJOU-KUN, HERE, WAS KIND ENOUGH TO COME PERFORM HIS SONG FOR OUR UPCOMING COMPETITION. HE'S DOING IT LIVE FOR US.

NOT SO FAST. WHERE ARE YOU GOING? YOU'RE SKATING ALONG WITH HIS PERFORM-ANCE.

EWW, WHAT'S UP WITH THE ATTITUDE, ANYWAY?

WHAT A CREEP.

WHAT ?!

8

11

13

CLAMP SCHOOL DEFENDERS DUKLYON

Introduction:

The CLAMP School is Japan's top learning institution and home to geniuses and wunderkinds of every make and model. For the little problems, like lost pets and damsels in distress, the CLAMP School Detectives are on the case, but bigger crimes call for bigger crime fighters. Enter Duklyon: the CLAMP School Defenders. Kentaro and Takeshi aren't your typical superheroes, though. In fact, if they didn't have the fearsome taskmaster Eri on their backs all the time, they probably wouldn't go through the trouble. But when an intergalactic mastermind bent on world domination takes root in the CLAMP School, the Duklyon team is in action and on the case.

Created by: CLAMP

CLAMP is the all-female manga creative team made up of Nanase Ohkawa, Mokona Apapa, Nekoi Mick, and Satsuki Igarashi. They started off as doujinshi (fan comics) manga creators, but their unique style and great stories caught the attention of several major publishers. Soon their comics were being published in the most popular manga magazines in Japan. CLAMP's unique style bridges the gap between boys and girls comics, making them one of the most sought-after groups in Japan.

Features:

From the creators of *Chobits, Miyuki-Chan in Wonderland, Shirahime Syo,* and *Tokyo Babylon*

Free color poster included

Release date: Vol. 1 - 09/16/03
Vol. 2 - 11/11/03

Genre
Comedy/ Action

SRP: $9.99

18

EXCUSE ME. YOU TWO WERE HAVING SUCH A GOOD TIME, IT WAS HARD NOT TO EAVESDROP.

heh heh heh

I PREPARE A SCRUMPTIOUS BENTO BOX FOR YOU AND THIS IS THE THANKS I GET?!

KOTOBUKI SUKIYABASHI
CLAMP School High School Freshman,
Homeroom Z

SCREW YOU! YOU AND I ARE HERE TO DEFEND THE PEACE!

YOU'VE GOT THE WRONG IDEA, PAL. I DON'T KNOW THIS LOSER.

WHO'S HAVING A GOOD TIME?

YOU AND HIGASHIKUNIMARU-KUN.

DON'T MIND HIM, SUKIYABASHI. HE SOMETIMES STARTS RANDOMLY SPEWING NONSENSE.

MMFF MFFPH

WE'RE THE CLAMP SCHOOL DEFENDERS DUK—!!

ARE YOU DRUNK?! YOU IDIOT!

DUKLYON

20

DUKLYON

WHAT'S WRONG, SUKIYA-BASHI!?

I'M SORRY. I DON'T FEEL WELL. MAY I GO TO THE NURSE'S OFFICE?

NO WAY!

AND SO IF WE INSERT X-SQUARED HERE--

IT'S CLEAR YOU TWO ARE BEST FRIENDS.

IT'S OKAY. I'M FINE.

I'M SORRY TO HEAR THAT. SHUKAIDO AND HIGASHIKUNI-MARU, SINCE YOU TWO ARE ON THE STUDENT BODY HEALTH BOARD, CAN ONE OF YOU ESCORT HIM TO THE NURSE?

LOOK, I'M SPINNING FOR THE RECORD.

SIR, PLEASE DON'T LUMP ME IN WITH THIS WASTEOID.

IT'S TOO BAD YOU TWO CAN'T SHARE SOME OF YOUR RESTLESS ENERGY.

SUKIYA-BASHI LOOKS TERRIBLY ANEMIC.

I WOULDN'T WANT TO DISRUPT THEIR VALUABLE EDUCATION.

IF YOU HANG IT BY THE WINDOW,

I WON'T SLEEP TONIGHT.

IF YOU STUDENTS ARE GOING TO INTERRUPT...

WHAT IS THAT MUSIC? IT'S OFF-PUTTING, YET STRANGELY ALLURING!

WHAT'S GOING ON?!

MATHEMATICS

LET'S CONTINUE THEN.

IF WE INSERT X-SQUARED HERE.

SIR!

WE'RE NOT FEELING WELL, EITHER! MAY WE GO TO THE NURSE'S OFFICE TOO?!

UH... OKAY.

SO, WHAT'S THE SITUATION?

IN THE OLD DAYS, A CRIMINAL WOULD **NEVER** HAVE KIDNAPPED A CHILD FROM KINDERGARTEN!

THERE'S NO HONOR LEFT IN THIS WORLD.

A KIDNAPPER?! WHAT A SLEAZE!

HAS THE WORLD GONE MAD? A KID IS SNATCHED FROM KINDERGARTEN WHILE ALL THE OTHER CLASSES GO ON UNDISTURBED!

SPECIAL RESCUE POLICE WINSPECTOR SAYS THE SAME THING!

ROBOTIC DETECTIVE JIBAN ALWAYS SAID THE HEAVIEST PUNISHMENTS ARE RESERVED FOR THOSE WHO WOULD DESTROY A CHILD'S DREAMS!

LET ME GO! LET ME GOOO!

CLAMP SCHOOL KINDERGARTEN

The evil secret society: **THE IMONOYAMA SHOPPING DISTRICT ASSOCIATION**

TO BE CONTINUED...

28

FLCL

Introduction:

From the twisted mind of Gainax (*Evangelion, Kare Kano*) comes this bizarre tale of adolescence in a non-sensical world. Naota's life isn't simple. He lives with his eccentric father and grandfather in a city whose most distinguishing landmark is a gigantic hand-iron shaped factory perched on a hill. The last thing he needs is for his brother's ex-girlfriend to make passes at him, or for an impish, playful alien to smack him in the head with a bass guitar and then insinuate herself into his family. And that's just the beginning of it.

Created by: Gainax

In the vast lineup of anime creative team Gainax, *FLCL* is the brainchild of Tsurumaki-san, the young director that brought to life the *End of Evangelion*, a miasmic animated adventure. The manga was written by Hajime Ueda and adapted from the anime.

Features:

Manga based on the hit anime from Studio Gainax, creators of *Neon Genesis Evangelion* (as seen on Cartoon Network)

Appeals to fans of *Cowboy Bebop* and *Mahoromatic: Automatic Maiden*

Release date: Vol. 1 - 09/16/03
Vol. 2 - 11/04/03

Genre
Action/Adventure/
Sci-Fi
SRP: $9.99

Sunday

That's right. Lift those boxes. Since you don't have any nifty functions you can at least lend some muscle around the house.

Oh, you think he's all yours because you found him?

What a selfish attitude!

You're using him outside again? The neighbors have eyes, you know!

Nao, check the scorebook...

I found him?

Besides, who cares what people think? So there's a robot in the house. It just irds you out because it's shaped like a person and you don't like new people. It's all about...

31

35

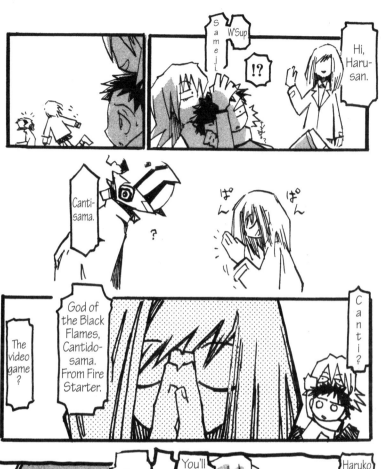

H
m
p
h!

Grandpa didn't like Mamimi dating my brother.

What's his problem?

Why do you care, anyway?! Leggo already!

To Be Continued...

Forbidden Dance

Introduction:

When a young girl loses her confidence to dance, she fears she'll never set foot on the stage again. But then she falls in lust with an all-guy avant-garde dance troupe and their leader...and everything changes. Soon, her primary goal in life is to join the troupe and snag the guy. So what if she's missing a Y-chromosome? She's got spunk, skill, and passion—and, in the end, she hopes that love will conquer all.

FORBIDDEN DANCE

Created by: Hinako Ashihara

Hinako Ashihara is the creator of *Girls Lesson, Homemade Home, Hoshifuru Heya de, Derby Queen, Miss, Tennen Bitter Chocolate,* and *Yubikiri.*

Features:

A manga that combines female teen angst and the world of dance

A top shojo manga from the creator of seven series since 1994

Release date:

Vol. 1 - 08/05/03
Vol. 2 - 10/07/03
Vol. 3 - 01/06/04
Vol. 4 - 03/02/04

Genre
Romance

SRP: $9.99

主催・
バレエ・コンクー
Ballet · Concou

YOU'LL BE GREAT! DO YOUR BEST AS USUAL AND YOU WILL WIN THIS COMPETITION.

GOOD LUCK, AYA!

NUMBER 16.

AYA FUJII FROM MACHIDA BALLET SCHOOL.

TAP

YES?

43

I have the same nightmare every night.

A month has passed since the competition.

NACHAN!

I HAVEN'T SEEN YOU FOR A WHILE! GOOD TO HAVE YOU BACK!!

AYA!

I CAN'T TAKE A BREAK FOREVER, YOU KNOW.

BESIDES, THE NEXT RECITAL IS SOON.

I AM SO HAPPY TO SEE YOU. WE WERE ALL SO WORRIED ABOUT YOU!!

48

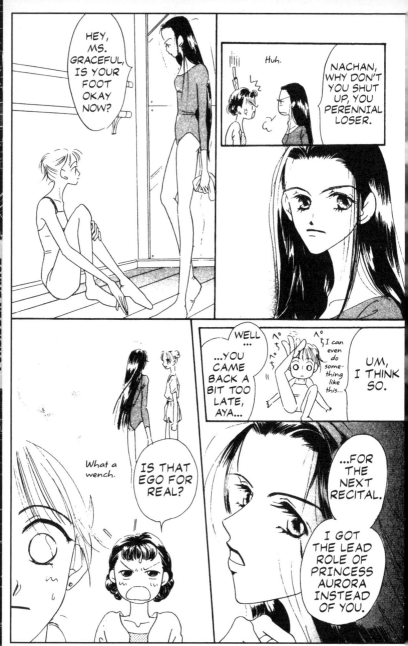

AYA, YOSHINO GOT THE ROLE OF AURORA?

IT'S NOT FAIR.

I WAS REALLY HOPING TO PLAY PRINCESS AURORA IN *SLEEPING BEAUTY*.

THERE'S NOTHING I CAN DO ABOUT IT.

I WAS OFF FOR A MONTH AFTER ALL.

Ballet Mast

JUST AS I TOLD YOU, YOSHINO...

BUT... I DON'T UNDERSTAND!!

MS. GRACEFUL? WHY?

I CAN'T ACCEPT THAT!! I CAN DO BETTER THAN SOMEONE WHO HASN'T EVEN BEEN TRAINING FOR A MONTH!!

NOW THAT AYA IS COMPLETELY RECOVERED...

...SHE IS GOING TO DANCE THE PART OF PRINCESS AURORA AS ORIGINALLY PLANNED.

I HAVE THE FINAL SAY ON CASTING.

IF YOU WANT THE LEAD PART, YOU NEED TO TRAIN HARDER AND IMPROVE YOUR TECHNIQUE.

HUSH, YOSHINO.

HELLO?! I AM THE DANCER WHO WON THE COMPETITION!! I DIDN'T CHOKE UNDER PRESSURE!

51

MIYUKI-CHAN in
WONDERLAND

Introduction:

There are many worlds in the universe outside of our
own, connected by doors that are hidden to the eye.
But if you chance upon those doors, you can be
transported to a place where supple beauties reign
supreme and all of your fantasies come alive. Should
you pass through the doorways, be most careful, for
the creatures you will meet can be as dangerous as
they are beautiful. Many would die for a glimpse at
those worlds, but Miyuki would do anything to have
them go away.

Created by: CLAMP

CLAMP is the all-female manga creative
team made up of Nanase Ohkawa, Mokona
Apapa, Nekoi Mick, and Satsuki Igarashi.
They started off as doujinshi (fan
comics) manga creators, but their unique
style and great stories caught the attention of several major publishers. Soon
their comics were being published in the
most popular manga magazines in Japan.
CLAMP's unique style bridges the gap
between boys and girls comics, making
them one of the most sought-after groups
in Japan.

Features:

From the creators of *Chobits, Miyuki-Chan
in Wonderland, Shirahime Syo,* and *Tokyo
Babylon*

24 pages of color art

Release date: Vol. 1 - 10/07/03

Genre
Comedy/ Fantasy

SRP: $9.99

61

TO BE CONTINUED...

PLANETES

Introduction:

In the near future, mankind's colonization of space is imminent—there are several orbital space stations, a few cities on the moon and plans are already being drafted for a manned outer solar system research mission. This is the exciting frontier that young Hachimaki longs to be a part of. Instead, he works as an orbital garbage man. He and his team are responsible for clearing away the glut of space junk mankind's foray into space has left in its wake. His team includes Fee, a spitfire, nicotine-addicted tomboy beauty with an abrasive edge; and Yuri, a veteran space man with a tragic past in search for inner peace. Planetes follows the lives of these three debris-men as they work and ruminate at the edge of the great empyrean sea.

Created by: Makoto Yukimura

Makoto Yukimura's most famous work, Planetes, started in Kodansha's weekly comic magazine *Morning* in 1999 when Yukimura was just 22 years old. Attracted to sci-fi writers such as Robert Heinlein and Jules Verne, Yukimura has always been fascinated with space and the potential to get there. Yukimura has become known for the heartfelt 'ordinariness' of his approach to life in space and the depth of the characterization he achieves in his painstakingly-beautiful illustrations.

Features:

Manga that inspired the new anime hit from Sunrise

Appeals to fans of *Gundam*

Genre
Action/Adventure/Sci-fi

SRP: $9.99

Release date: Vol. 1 - 10/07/03 Vol. 2 - 01/06/04
Vol. 3 - 06/01/04

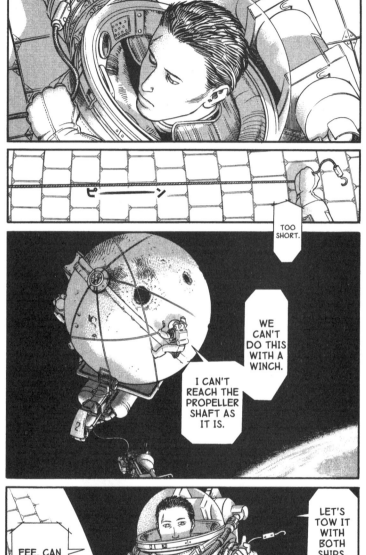

ピーン

TOO SHORT.

WE CAN'T DO THIS WITH A WINCH.

I CAN'T REACH THE PROPELLER SHAFT AS IT IS.

FEE, CAN YOU COME A LITTLE CLOSER?

LET'S TOW IT WITH BOTH SHIPS.

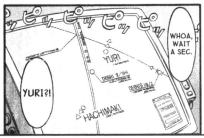

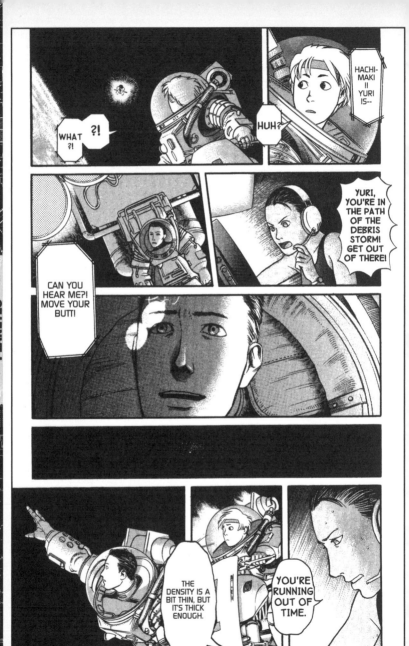

72

TOKYOPOP
PSYCHIC ACADEMY™
You don't have to be a great psychic to be a great hero
. . . but it helps.
Available March 2004 At Your Favorite Book And Comic Stores.
T
TEEN
AGE 13+
www.TOKYOPOP.com
© 1999 Katsu Aki All Rights Reserved.

SHIRAHIME-SYO

SHIRAHIME-SYO

Introduction:

Legends say that when it snows, it is because
the snow princess is crying. From CLAMP, creators
of *Chobits and Cardcaptor Sakura*, comes a
collection of five tragic tales, all connected by
the bond of snow. *Shirahime-syo* is CLAMP's return
to traditional Japanese form and storytelling.
Featuring luscious watercolors and gentle brush-
strokes, it is a beautiful departure from CLAMP's
usual fare. Discover for yourself the mystery
behind the snow.

Created by: CLAMP

CLAMP is the all-female manga creative
team made up of Nanase Ohkawa, Mokona
Apapa, Nekoi Mick, and Satsuki Igarashi.
They started off as doujinshi (fan
comics) manga creators but their unique
style and great stories caught the attention of several major publishers. Soon
their comics were being published in the
most popular manga magazines in Japan.
CLAMP's unique style bridges the gap
between boys and girls comics,
making them one of the most sought-
after groups in Japan.

Features:

Deluxe hardcover edition and paperback
edition available

From the creators of *Chobits, Miyuki-Chan
in Wonderland, Shirahime Syo,* and *Tokyo
Babylon*

Release date: Vol. 1 - 12/09/03

Genre
Fantasy

SRP:
Hardcover $19.99
Softcover $9.99

TEEN
AGE 13+

牙狼の山

ON WOLF MOUNTAIN

がろうのやま

82

TO BE CONTINUED...

88

STOP!

You wouldn't want to spoil a great ending!

The rest of this book is printed "manga-style," in the authentic Japanese right-to-left format. Turn the book over and start again. Since none of the artwork has been flipped or altered, readers get to experience the story just as the creator intended. You've been asking for it, so TOKYOPOP® delivered: authentic, hot-off-the-press, and far more fun!

DIRECTIONS

If this is your first time reading manga-style, here's a quick guide to help you understand how it works.

It's easy... just start in the top right panel and follow the numbers. Have fun, and look for more 100% authentic manga from TOKYOPOP®!

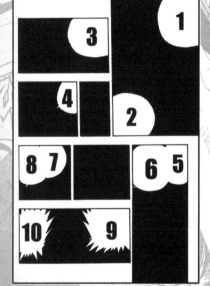

2003 RELEASE SCHEDULE

BOOKS

September Releases

.hack//Legend of the Twilight, Vol.1
Baby Birth, Vol.1
Battle Royale, Vol.3
Chronicles of the Cursed Sword, Vol.2
Confidential Confessions, Vol.2
Cyborg 009, Vol.1
Demon Diary, Vol.3
Duklyon: CLAMP School Defenders, Vol.1
Erica Sakurazawa: Angel Nest
FAKE, Vol.3
FLCL, Vol.1
GTO, Vol.14
Kare Kano, Vol.5
Kim Possible Cine-Manga, Vol.3
Kodocha: Sana's Stage, Vol.9
Lizzie McGuire Cine-Manga, Vol.2
Love Hina, Vol.14
Lupin III, Vol.7
Mars, Vol.14
Peach Girl: Change of Heart, Vol.4
Priest, Vol.8
Rebirth, Vol.4
Saber Marionette J, Vol.2
Scryed, Vol.4
Spongebob Squarepants, Vol.1
Stray Sheep Picture Book
Stray Sheep Poe At Play
Stray Sheep Merry on The Move
Stray Sheep Plush Dolls Small Poe Plush
Stray Sheep Plush Dolls Small Merry Plush
The Adventures of Jimmy Neutron: Boy Genius
The Vision of Escaflowne, Vol.2
Under The Glass Moon, Vol.2
Wild Act, Vol.2
Zodiac P.I., Vol.2

October Releases

@ Large
Brain Powered, Vol.3
Brigadoon, Vol.2
Cardcaptor Sakura Boxed Set Volume 1: Collection 1
Chobits, Vol.8
Chobits, Vol.8 w/special edition Chi figurine
Cowboy Bebop: Boxed Set The Complete Collection
Dragon Hunter, Vol.3
Dragon Knights, Vol.10
Forbidden Dance, Vol.2
G Gundam, Vol.3
G.I. Joe, Vol.1
Gravitation, Vol.2
Happy Mania, Vol.4
Initial D, Vol.8
Jing: King of Bandits, Vol.3
King of Hell, Vol.3
Lupin III, Vol.8
Magic Knight Rayearth I, Vol.2
Miyuki-chan in Wonderland
Pet Shop of Horrors, Vol.3
Planetes, Vol.1
Ragnarok, Vol.8
Rave Master, Vol.5
Rebound, Vol.4
Samurai Deeper Kyo, Vol.3
Shaolin Sisters, Vol.5
Shutterbox, Vol.1
The Kindaichi Case Files, Vol.3 Death TV
Tokyo Mew Mew, Vol.4
Transformers: Armada, Vol.1
Transformers: Armada, Vol.2
Vampire Game, Vol.3
World of Hartz
X-Day, Vol.2

November Releases

Baby Birth, Vol.2
Battle Royale, Vol.4
Chronicles of the Cursed Sword, Vol.3
Confidential Confessions, Vol.3
Cyborg 009, Vol.2
Demon Diary, Vol.4
Duklyon: CLAMP School Defenders, Vol.2
Erica Sakurazawa: Nothing But Loving You
FAKE, Vol.4
Finding Nemo
FLCL, Vol.2
GTO, Vol.15
Jackie Chan Adventures, Vol.1
Kare Kano, Vol.6